Landmark
Events in
American
History

The Salem
Witch Trials

Michael V. Uschan

WORLD ALMANAC® LIBRARY

Dedication
To Carole Grove, Mary Horton, and Barbara Bates

Please visit our web site at: www.worldalmanaclibrary.com
For a free color catalog describing World Almanac® Library's list of high-quality
books and multimedia programs, call 1-800-848-2928 (USA) or 1-800-387-3178
(Canada). World Almanac® Library's fax: (414) 332-3567.

Library of Congress Cataloging-in-Publication Data available upon request from publisher.
Fax (414) 336-0157 for the attention of the Publishing Records Department.

ISBN 0-8368-5387-3 (lib. bdg.)
ISBN 0-8368-5415-2 (softcover)

First published in 2004 by
World Almanac® Library
330 West Olive Street, Suite 100
Milwaukee, WI 53212 USA

Produced by Discovery Books
Editor: Sabrina Crewe
Designer and page production: Sabine Beaupré
Photo researcher: Sabrina Crewe
Maps and diagrams: Stefan Chabluk
World Almanac® Library editorial direction: Mark J. Sachner
World Almanac® Library art direction: Tammy Gruenewald
World Almanac® Library production: Jessica Morris

Photo credits: Corbis: pp. 4, 5, 6, 8, 11, 12, 14, 16, 17, 19, 21, 24, 29, 30, 31, 34, 35,
36–37, 42, 43; North Wind Picture Archives: cover, pp. 7, 9, 10, 13, 15, 18, 22, 23, 25,
26, 27, 28, 32, 33, 38, 39, 40, 41.

Printed in the United States of America

1 2 3 4 5 6 7 8 9 08 07 06 05 04

Contents

Introduction

Salem Village and Salem Town

Although the accusations of witchcraft started in Salem Village, the Salem Witch Trials took place in Salem Town. Founded in 1626, Salem Town was a port city located on the coast of the Atlantic Ocean. It was the first permanent settlement in the Massachusetts Bay **Colony**. In the late 1630s, people began moving inland from Salem Town to become farmers. The community that grew up as a result, some 5 miles (8 km) west of Salem Town, became known as Salem Village. By 1672, Salem Village had built its own **meeting house** and had its own minister. Salem Village is now called Danvers, and Salem Town is known simply as Salem. Both are in the state of Massachusetts.

A view of Danvers (formerly Salem Village) in about 1850.

Salem Village

Danvers, Massachusetts, is a small town of 24,000 people located 17 miles (27 kilometers) north of Boston. In this pleasant community are over a dozen houses dating back to the seventeenth century, when the town was known as Salem Village. The houses are a direct link to one of the most sensational and unfortunate events in colonial American history: the Salem Witch **Trials**. It was in Salem Village that, in 1692, several young girls first accused people in their community of being witches.

Fear

People in Western society today do not, on the whole, believe in witches, but the men, women, and children who lived in Salem Village in 1692 did. They thought witches received magical powers from the devil, and they feared them because witches were believed to harm and even kill ordinary people. In seventeenth-century America, this terror of witches was very powerful. It was so great that the people of Salem Village did

This is one of the houses in Salem that has been preserved from the days of the Salem Witch Trials. Now known as the "Witch House," it was the home of Jonathan Corwin, one of the judges in the trials.

nothing when their friends, neighbors, and even relatives were accused of **witchcraft**, put in jail, and killed. They were simply too afraid of the witches. Many were also afraid that they themselves would be accused of witchcraft.

Within just a few months of the first accusations, 144 men and women had been imprisoned, accused of being witches. Before this strange episode had ended, 20 people had been executed. At least 4 others died while in prison—some historians believe it was as many as 13, including an infant born to a suspected witch.

An Army of Devils
"An Army of Devils is horribly broke in upon the place and the Houses of the Good People there are filled with the doleful Shrieks of their Children and Servants, Tormented by Invisible Hands, with Tortures altogether [supernatural]."

Reverend Cotton Mather, The Wonders of the Invisible World,
an account of witchcraft in Salem Village, 1693

Witches

A woodcut of a "black" witch and a "white" witch. According to folklore, witches wore tall pointed hats and were often accompanied by demons in the shape of animals, known as "familiars."

Good and Bad Magic

In earlier times, it was common for people living in many parts of the world to believe in magic and in witches. It was thought some witches did good things through "white" magic, such as healing sick people or helping crops to grow. Others were suspected of performing "black" magic, which harmed people or caused bad things to happen, such as violent storms or outbreaks of disease. Male witches were called wizards or sorcerers.

The Christian Fear of Magic

Jews, Muslims, and Christians all believe in one god who symbolizes goodness. Many earlier religions, known as **pagan** religions,

Why People Believed in Magic

People used to believe in magic because they could not understand many things that happened to them or in the world around them. Today, if a long drought destroys crops or a terrible disease kills many people, there is a scientific explanation for it. But when such calamities happened three hundred years ago, people had no idea what caused them. Because they could not explain why or how such things occurred, they attributed them to gods, devils, or just the mysterious force of magic.

worshiped multiple gods and other things, such as natural forces. The belief in magic was central to pagan religions, and Christians particularly disliked and feared anyone who practiced magic. They believed that anyone with magic powers received them from the devil, not from God.

In the 1400s, Roman Catholic saint Thomas Aquinas wrote that the devil invented magic to tempt people away from Christianity. And Martin Luther, who in the sixteenth century led a Christian movement to create the **Protestant** faith, also claimed that all witches were evil. Christians believed that witches should be put to death, and they used several passages in the Bible to justify this belief. The key one is in Exodus 22:17, which proclaims, "Thou shall not suffer a witch to live."

Hunting Witches

From the fifteenth to seventeenth centuries, Christians waged a war against witches in Europe. Roman Catholic and Protestant church officials hunted, jailed, and killed hundreds of thousands of people who were suspected of being witches.

An **edict** that gave the stamp of approval to witch-hunting was issued by Pope Innocent VIII, leader of the Catholic

Sixteenth-century Protestant leader Martin Luther believed firmly in witches. Like many Christians, he thought people who appeared to have special powers were associated with the devil.

Raising Storms and Riding Broomsticks
"[They] are the Devil's [partners] who steal milk, raise storms, ride on broomsticks, lame or maim people, torture babies in their cradles, change things into different shapes."

Protestant leader Martin Luther, speaking about witches in a sermon, 1521

Burning was the usual method of executing witches in Europe. This woodcut shows a suspected witch being burned to death in Germany in 1555.

Church, in 1484. Pope Innocent claimed that men and women who "gave themselves over to devils male and female" were witches and should be found and killed. The Pope was strongly influenced by Catholic priests Jakob Sprenger and Heinrich Kramer, who were witch experts. In 1486, the two wrote *Malleus Maleficarum*, Latin for "The Hammer of Witches." In addition to explaining what witches were and detailing the powers they had, the book set down procedures for trying suspected witches. This work was so popular that for many decades people bought more copies of it than any other book except the Bible.

Helped by the Devil

"It is a most certain opinion that there are sorcerers and witches who by the help of the Devil, on account of a compact which they have entered into with him, are able to produce real and actual evils and harm."

Catholic priests Jakob Sprenger and Heinrich Kramer, Malleus Maleficarum, 1486

Beliefs About Witches

The vast majority of people accused of being witches in Salem Village and elsewhere were women. This was because men considered women weaker and inferior and therefore more likely to be ensnared by the devil. Witches were said to be able to change their appearance to look like animals or other people, and they could fly through the air on broomsticks. They harmed people by casting spells over them, and they were aided by demons that took the shape of cats and other small animals. This type of demon, or evil spirit, was called a familiar. Apparently, witches were unable to swim, weep, or recite the Lord's Prayer.

The people of Salem believed they could identify witches by several methods. For instance, villager Mary Sibley once collected the urine of children who claimed to be affected by witches. She baked it with rye flour to make a witch cake, which she fed to a dog. The dog was supposed to go to the witch who was affecting the girls, but instead it just got sick.

Another way to identify a witch was to find an unusual mark, such as a mole or wart, on his or her body. It was believed the devil used such spots on a witch's body to feed and draw energy. In Salem, when five-year-old Dorcas Good was found to have a red spot on the tip of her finger, it was considered proof that she was a witch, and she was imprisoned.

An illustration of a witch performing spells shows three black cats, the witch's familiars.

The Puritans

In England, King Henry VIII issued an edict in 1542 that banned witchcraft. Then, in 1604, the English government passed a Witchcraft Act that ordered death for convicted witches.

When English settlers of the period moved to North America, they took their fear of witches with them. The **Puritans** were among the first English settlers in the land that would one day become the United States. The term "Puritan" refers to a Protestant group that opposed some practices of the Anglican Church, then England's official religion. Puritans wanted to purify, or rid, the Anglican Church of Roman Catholic traditions. Some Puritans, known as Separatists, felt strongly enough to separate from the Church of England altogether.

In 1620, a group of Separatist Puritans landed in North America at a site that is now Plymouth, Massachusetts. Later known as the "Pilgrims," the Plymouth colonists were the first of thousands of Puritans who would settle **New England**. Other Puritans arriving soon after the Plymouth colonists founded the Massachusetts Bay Colony, which grew rapidly in the 1600s and absorbed Plymouth Colony before the end of the century.

The first European settlers in New England were the Puritans of Plymouth Colony, shown here in the 1620s in the meeting house that was their place of worship.

For those who failed to conform to Puritan society, there were a number of humiliating punishments. This suspected witch is being plunged into the village pond on a device, made for that purpose, called a ducking stool.

Witches in Massachusetts

In its early days, the Massachusetts Bay Colony was controlled by the leaders of the Puritan Church, who were vigilant about hunting down supposed witches in their midst. When they found them, church officials punished but did not always kill accused witches.

For most of the seventeenth century, there were only scattered cases of witchcraft in New England. The first witch trial in the Massachusetts Bay Colony occurred in 1648, when Margaret Jones of Charlestown was hanged after being found guilty of being a witch. The most serious charge against her was that some people the woman touched had died. Jones was a midwife, however, someone who assisted other women when they had babies. She also was a healer who tried to help sick people get better. It would seem normal that some people she had contact with would die, in the days when many women died in childbirth and disease **epidemics** spread with no medicines to stop them. There were more witch trials over the next forty years in New England, but they were few and far between until 1692.

A Malignant Touch

"The evidence against [Margaret Jones] was that she was found to have a malignant [evil] touch as many persons (men, women, and children) who she stroked or touched with any affection or displeasure or, etc., were taken with deafness, or vomiting, or other violent pains or sickness. . . . The same day and hour she was executed, there was a very great tempest which blew down many trees, etc."

The journal of John Winthrop, governor of Massachusetts Bay Colony during Margaret Jones's trial in 1648

Chapter 2

The Accusations Begin

A New Pastor

In 1689, the Reverend Samuel Parris became pastor of the Church of Christ in Salem Village. Formerly a merchant on the Caribbean island of Barbados, he brought his family to Salem with him: his wife Elizabeth, daughter Elizabeth, and niece Abigail Williams.

A Girl's Life in Colonial New England

Basic household tasks took up much of the day in colonial New England.

The Puritans founded public schools in larger communities because they wanted everyone to read so they could study the Bible. But many colonial children, especially girls, were taught to read and write at home, if at all.

Domestic work took up most of the hours of the day as there were no labor-saving machines and electrical power, and nearly all food and clothing was produced rather than bought. Even young girls like Elizabeth Parris and Abigail Williams had to do chores, such as hauling water, washing clothes, and making candles. Colonial children collected fruit and nuts, looked after farm animals, and worked in the fields. Prayer, worship, and Bible study filled the time when they weren't working or sleeping.

In the few moments left for fun, colonial children could play outside in summer. In winter, however, the cold kept Abigail and Elizabeth indoors, with just their imaginations and stories about witchcraft for amusement.

In this illustration of Tituba telling stories of witchcraft, she is shown as old and witch-like. In fact, she was probably quite young. She may have admitted to being a witch because she practiced fortune-telling, which was considered "white magic."

Tituba and the Girls

Reverend Parris brought two slaves—Tituba and John Indian—with him to Salem Village. (It was unusual for people in New England to own slaves, although slave labor was becoming common in American colonies of the South.) The girls in the Parris household and their friends often amused themselves in the winter of 1691–1692 by listening to Tituba Indian's exciting stories of life in Barbados. The slave told tales of magic and how to tell the future. One way to predict the future was to put egg white into a glass of water. The shape the egg white took was supposed to foretell what would happen to the person. Once when the girls did this, they saw the shape of a coffin, which scared them.

Strange Behavior

In late January 1692, nine-year-old Elizabeth and eleven-year-old Abigail began acting strangely. They screamed during church services, had seizures in which their limbs thrashed about violently, went into trance-like states, fainted, and made strange faces. In February, other girls who were friends of Elizabeth and Abigail began exhibiting similar behavior. They included seventeen-year-old Elizabeth Hubbard and twelve-year-old Ann Putnam.

This is a replica of the meeting house in Salem Village where the women accused of witchcraft were questioned by local magistrates. The replica stands in Danvers today.

Parris was unable to stop the bizarre behavior through prayer, so he consulted a village physician. When Doctor William Griggs could not find anything physically wrong with the girls, he concluded, "The evil hand is upon them." Griggs meant that the devil or witches were causing the girls to act strangely.

The First Charges

Fearing that witches were responsible, Parris and other adults in late February began pressuring the girls to reveal who was attacking them. Elizabeth and Abigail refused to name anyone. But when the questioning continued, they finally accused three villagers: Tituba Indian, Sarah Good, and Sarah Osborne.

On February 29, the three were arrested on suspicion of being witches. They and other suspected witches became known as the accused. The girls who made the claims were called the **afflicted**.

The Investigation Begins

On March 1, 1692, the three accused were questioned in the Salem Village meeting house by two **magistrates**, Jonathan Corwin and

Tituba Indian

One of the most interesting figures in the Salem Witch Trials was Tituba Indian. She and her husband John Indian were slaves whom Reverend Parris bought when he lived on the Caribbean island of Barbados. An Arawak Indian from South America, Tituba was captured as a child, taken to Barbados, and sold into slavery. Although Tituba Indian's admission that she was a witch was a key factor in the explosion of fear that led to the Salem Witch Trials, she later claimed Parris had beaten her to make her confess she was a witch. After the witch trials ended in 1693, Tituba Indian was released from prison and then sold. It is not known what happened to her after that.

15

Puritan Rule

For Puritans in New England, absolute **conformity** in all aspects of life was required. Puritans had no tolerance for religions beside their own. They believed religion was the most important factor in society—church leaders led the community and set its strict moral standards. In addition, male church members were the only ones who could make local government decisions at town meetings. In these ways, the Puritans kept control of the people of New England for many years.

Men and women who engaged in behavior that did not conform to Puritan ideals, such as failing to attend church regularly, were considered immoral. Such people, already outcasts because they did not conform, were among the first to be accused of being witches.

A Puritan family gives thanks at the dinner table.

John Hathorne. Osborne and Good denied they were witches. Tituba Indian denied she hurt the girls, but then she shocked listeners by admitting she was a witch. Especially riveting was her **testimony** of how witches rode brooms: "We ride upon a stick or pole. Don't know how we go, for I saw no trees nor path, but was presently there." Indian also claimed Good and Osborne were witches. The women were charged with witchcraft and imprisoned in nearby Boston.

Specters

A key to determining whether the women should be charged was a type of testimony known as spectral **evidence**. It was believed the devil allowed witches to use **specters** in their own shape to harm

Sightings of specters increased along with accusations of witchcraft. In this illustration of a witch trial in the 1600s, the women seated are pointing to a flock of birds they claim to see above an accused witch.

The Questioning of Sarah Good

Judges: "What evil spirit have you familiarity with?"

Good: "None."

Judges: "Have you made no contract with the devil?"

Good: "No."

Judges: Why do you hurt these children?

Good: "I do not hurt them. I scorn it [witchcraft]."

Judges: "Who do you imploy [use] then to do it?"

Good: "I imploy no body."

Judges: "What creature do you imploy then?"

Good: "No creature. I am falsely accused."

Examination of Sarah Good by magistrates John Hathorne and Jonathan Corwin, March 1692

Martha Corey, seen here on trial for witchcraft in 1692, was an outspoken woman. She was one of the few people brave enough to oppose the witch trials from the beginning, which is probably why she was accused.

people from a distance. The afflicted claimed that the specters of the three accused witches were flying through the air, biting and pinching them. Because a specter was a spirit visible only to the afflicted, however, there was no way to prove specters were real.

More Charges

The first charges of witchcraft in March 1692 were quickly followed by many more. In the next few weeks, other girls and even some adults made accusations against other villagers. Once again, spectral evidence was used to condemn some people. One day in April, while in church, Reverend Parris's niece Abigail Williams cried out, "Look where Goodwife [Martha] Corey sits upon the beam [with] her yellow bird between her fingers." Corey was seated in a pew in the church at the time. But the girl's claim that Corey's specter was hovering high above churchgoers, accompanied by a familiar, was considered proof she was a witch.

The people of Salem Village lived in fear of a sudden accusation. In this scene, a girl clings to her father as she is accused of being a witch.

19

The Witch Trials

This map shows Massachusetts and adjacent colonies in the 1690s. Soon, accusations of witchcraft had spread out from Salem Village to surrounding communities.

Witches Everywhere

By the end of April 1692, over two dozen suspects were in jail. Added to the ranks of the accused were Martha and Giles Corey, Rebecca Nurse, Elizabeth and John Proctor, and Bridget Bishop. Another accused was a five-year-old girl, Dorcas Good, who confessed in March, probably in order to join her mother, Sarah Good, in prison. Even George Burroughs, a former Salem Village pastor, was accused. When Deodat Lawson, also a former pastor in Salem, came to investigate the strange incidents, he wrote that "Satan Rages amongst the Visible Subjects of [the village] so that Christ's Kingdom may be divided against itself, and so be weakened."

The fear of witches soon spread to nearby communities, where people began to "discover" other witches in their midst. Suspected witches were uncovered in Salem Town, Andover, Salem Farmes, Beverly, Marblehead, and Boston. By the end of May 1692,

Testimony against Dorcas Good

"About [March 31] I saw the apparition of Sarah Good's daughter come to me and bit me and pinch me and so she continued afflicting me . . ."

Testimony of Mary Walcott, one of the afflicted,
April 1692

The Witches of Andover

In July 1692, nearly seventy suspected witches were discovered in Andover, northwest of Salem Village. The discovery of so many witches in one place came after Reverend Thomas Barnard became worried that many people in his town were sick, including his wife. Fearing witchcraft was causing the illness, Barnard invited Salem Village girls Ann Putnam and Mary Walcott to visit and spot the witches. The girls claimed that they saw specters hovering over the bodies of ill people in every home they visited. When the girls met with Andover women, they accused sixty-seven of them of being witches.

local jails were overflowing. Residents of New England soon believed scores of witches were living among them.

Types of Accused

The case of former pastor George Burroughs was an example of how the kind of people alleged to be witches began to change. At first, the accused were people whom villagers already looked down on because they seemed strange or did not conform in some way. Of the first three suspected witches, Tituba Indian was a slave, Sarah Good a poor woman who begged for food, and Sarah Osborne an eccentric old woman who did not attend church.

Because they were already outcasts, it was easy for people to believe they were evil. But Burroughs had been a religious leader in the Puritan Church. People charged with witchcraft in the past in New England had always had questionable reputations, but now respectable people were being accused, too.

The Court of Oyer and Terminer

Before anyone could be **tried**, the colony of Massachusetts had to wait for its new governor,

Just the word of an afflicted person was enough to claim another suspect. Once people were accused of witchcraft, they were arrested and taken to prison to await trial.

Witch Hill, or Gallows Hill, was a bare and rocky rise outside Salem Town. All the executed witches except for one met their deaths there.

Sir William Phips, to bring a **charter** from England. After Phips sailed into Boston Harbor on May 14, 1692, he wasted no time in setting up a court to deal with the witchcraft crisis.

Phips appointed a Court of Oyer and Terminer (*oyer* and *terminer* are Latin words that mean "to hear" and "to decide") to try accused witches. He named several magistrates to hear cases: Lieutenant Governor William Stoughton, Nathaniel Saltonstall, Bartholomew Gedney, Peter Sergeant, Samuel Sewall, Waitstill Winthrop, John Richards, John Hathorne, and Jonathan Corwin. The trials were held at the courthouse in Salem Town.

The first accused to be tried was Bridget Bishop, a Salem woman who had been tried and found innocent of being a witch in 1680.

A New Charter

Massachusetts was an English colony, and so the people who lived there were subjects of the English king. The king granted colonists permission to live in Massachusetts by issuing a charter, which also set out the basic laws governing the colony. A governor was appointed in England to run the colony. The charter for the colony had been cancelled in 1686, however, when residents refused to swear absolute obedience to the English Crown. In 1691, King William III of England finally granted a new charter, but it did not go into effect until May 1692, when Governor William Phips arrived to take power. So although the first accusations of witchcraft were made in February 1692, no trials were held until June—without a charter, local officials had no legal authority to hold trials. The delay in prosecuting the first cases contributed to the widespread growth of the fear that witches were everywhere.

In that earlier case, she had been accused of the death of a neighborhood child who mysteriously fell ill and died. The afflicted now claimed Bishop had used magic to kill many children.

In the trial in Salem on June 2, 1692, Bishop was found guilty by a **jury** of twelve citizens, despite her plea that "I am no witch. I am innocent. I know nothing of it." On June 10, Bishop was hanged. The hanging took place outside Salem at a place that soon became known as "Witch Hill" or "Gallows Hill."

Evil Dolls

One reason judges chose to try Bishop first was that she was the only suspect against whom they had any real evidence. Bishop had earlier hired two laborers to tear down cellar walls in her house. While working, John and William Bly had found several knotted rag dolls. Witches were known to use dolls as images of people, whom they could supposedly harm by sticking pins in the figures.

The dolls were enough to convict Bishop because the judges decided Bishop used them for evil purposes, even though she denied it. But at least the dolls were physical objects that could be seen and touched.

Spectral Evidence

Much of the evidence in the Salem Witch Trials was even less substantial than some rag dolls. Because judges relied so heavily on spectral evidence, people were being convicted simply because others said they saw specters of the accused. In the case of Giles Corey, for example, Ann Putnam **testified** that his specter kept tormenting her.

In the past, judges in New England witch trials had not

Giles Corey, shown here at his trial, was convicted purely on the spectral evidence of Ann Putnam. "I verily believe that Giles Corey is a dreadful wizard," she said, "for since he has been in prison he or his appearance has come to me a great many times and afflicted me."

The Danger of Speaking Out

Historians today believe some of the people in Salem Village were accused because they criticized the witch-hunt. Martha Corey, for example, had claimed openly—before she was accused—that the afflicted were "distracted girls" whose testimony was difficult to believe.

John Proctor, a prosperous Salem Village farmer and businessman, boasted he had cured his maid Mary Warren of odd behavior, such as the afflicted had shown, by threatening to beat her. He believed the afflicted were lying and warned they could "make devils of us all" with irresponsible charges.

When his wife, Elizabeth, also criticized the witch-hunt, she was charged; John Proctor was then accused of witchcraft when he came to her defense. Rebecca Nurse, an old Salem Village woman known for being kind to people, was also accused after saying, "I am troubled at some of their [accusations]. Some of the persons they have spoken of are, as I believe, as innocent as I."

allowed spectral evidence to play a decisive role. Now, however, this type of testimony became the focal point of most trials. Officials believed so firmly in specters that suspected witches were kept in chains, which was supposed to keep their spirits from roaming about to harm other people.

Rebecca Nurse was seventy-one years old when she was found guilty of being a witch. This is her house, still standing in Danvers.

The afflicted put on a dramatic show at the Salem Witch Trials. This scene from the trials shows one of the afflicted fallen to the floor, while the accused woman standing in front of the judges proclaims her innocence.

The Trials Continue

With local jails swelling with suspected witches, the Court of Oyer and Terminer resumed its trials. In proceedings on June 29 and 30, 1692, all five suspected witches who appeared before the court were found guilty: Sarah Good, Rebecca Nurse, Susannah Martin, Elizabeth Howe, and Sarah Wildes. Good had given birth while in prison, and her baby had died within a few weeks. In spite of the cold, miserable, and filthy conditions the infant had to endure in prison, the baby's death was added to her mother's alleged crimes.

The afflicted testified during the trials, often in spectacular fashion—they had fits, claimed to see specters hovering in the air, and screamed out loud that the suspects were torturing them by biting or pinching them. Nurse was found guilty even though thirty-nine neighbors signed a petition claiming she was a

Testimony Against Rebecca Nurse
"The apparition of Nurse told me she had killed Benjamin Holton and John Fuller and Rebekah Shepard, and she also told me that she and [two other witches] had killed young [Jonathan] Putnam's child. And immediately there did appear to me six children in winding [burial] sheets and they told me that they were my sister's children of Boston, and that Nurse and [two other witches] had murdered them, and charged me to go and tell these things to the magistrates or else they would tear me to pieces, for their blood did cry out for vengeance."

Testimony of Ann Putnam, mother of the afflicted Ann Putnam, March 1692

good Christian and that "we never had any cause or grounds to suspect her of any such thing as she is now accused of."

The Executions

The five were hanged on July 19. While Good was awaiting execution, Reverend Nicholas Noyes, the assistant minister of Salem Church, shouted at her that she was a witch. Good screamed back, "You are a liar! I am no more a witch than you are a wizard, and if you take away my life God will give you blood to drink!" According to Salem legend, when Noyes died twenty-five years later, he choked on his own blood.

In a third round of trials lasting from August 2 to August 6, another six people were convicted including Elizabeth Proctor, John Proctor, and George Burroughs. They were hanged on August 19, 1692.

Confessions and Silence

Although Burroughs and many others accused maintained their innocence until the end, at least forty-seven people confessed they were witches. Their confessions are suspect, however, because anyone who did confess was spared death. As Margaret Jacobs said, "They told me if I would not confess I should be put down into the dungeon and would be hanged, but if I would confess I should save my life." The reasoning was that anyone who confessed doing such a terrible thing must have repented, which meant they had broken free of the devil's control.

Nineteen of the twenty people executed for witch-craft at Salem in 1692 were hanged. They included George Burroughs, shown here. He was accused by the afflicted of being the leader of the Salem witches.

Executions in Puritan New England

By today's standards, the laws of the Massachusetts Bay Colony were extremely harsh. Witchcraft was just one of many offenses for which citizens could be put to death. A list of the colony's Capital Laws—having to do with crimes considered the most serious—prescribes death as a punishment for rape and murder, crimes still considered terrible today. Other offenses calling for death seem minor, however, such as sex outside of marriage or lying in a legal matter. The list of laws carrying the death penalty included references to passages in the Bible that justified the death sentence in the Puritan mind, such as the commandment to "honor thy father and mother." So even a person who would "curse or smite their natural father or mother" could be sentenced to death.

One accused, Giles Corey, refused twice to testify or even enter a plea of guilty or innocent. On September 19, officials took him to a field and began placing stones on his chest, a form of torture then common in England, used to make people confess to something. Corey refused to speak even then and was "pressed" to death.

This slab of stone is a memorial to Giles Corey. He was pressed to death because he refused to confess.

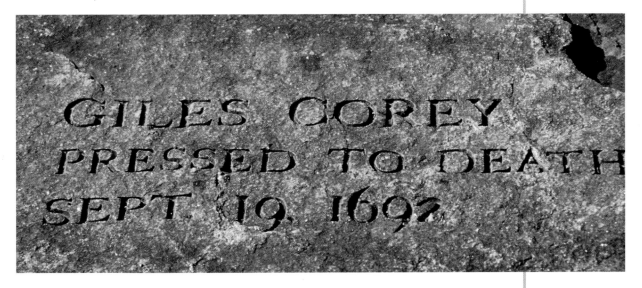

Outrageous Claims

The executions made some New Englanders feel safer, because they believed dangerous witches were being killed. But the frenzy over witches continued, and more and more people were charged. As time went by, it became hard to believe the outrageous claims that were being made. For instance, Susannah Post, an accused witch herself, claimed there were at least five hundred witches in New England. Mary Toothaker, another accused, said she had heard witches discuss "pulling down the kingdom of Christ and setting up the Kingdom of Satan." Suspicions arose that such exaggerated claims could not be true, and that threw

The judge stands to pronounce yet another sentence at the Salem Witch Trials. As the months went by, so many accused were being found guilty that people in Massachusetts began to have doubts.

No More Innocent Blood

"I know I must die, and my appointed time is set. But the Lord He knows it is, if it be possible, that no more innocent blood be shed, which undoubtedly cannot be avoided in the way and course you go in. I question not but your honors do to the utmost of your powers in the discovery and detecting of witchcraft and witches, and would not be guilty of innocent blood for the world. But by my own innocency I know you are in the wrong way. The Lord in his infinite mercy direct you in this great work, if it be His blessed will, that innocent blood be not shed . . ."

Mary Towne Easty, asking the judges to stop convicting innocent people, before she was hanged on September 22, 1692

doubt on the whole trial process.

It also became harder to believe that some of the people being accused could possibly be witches. Charges were made against many influential and respected people, including the wives of Governor Phips and Reverend Increase Mather, an influential minister who was also head of Harvard College in Massachusetts. People began asking themselves, could there be so many witches in New England? They also began wondering if the people already in jail or executed were really and truly witches.

The Ballad of Giles Corey
"Giles Corey was a wizard strong,
A stubborn wretch was he,
And fit was he to hang on high,
Upon the locust tree.

'Giles Corey,' said the magistrate,
'What have thou here to plead
To these who now accuse thy soul
Of crimes and horrid deed?'

Giles Corey—he said not a word,
No single word spoke he.
'Giles Corey,' said the magistrate,
'We'll press it out of thee.'

They got them then a heavy beam,
They laid it on his breast.
They loaded it with heavy stones,
And hard upon him pressed.

'More weight,' now said this wretched man,
'More weight,' again he cried.
And he did no confession make
But wickedly died."

A nineteenth-century song

The guilty verdicts continued even as the accused proclaimed their innocence. These memorial stones are carved with the words of those who died.

Doubts and Questions

By the fall of 1692, more than 200 people stood accused of witch-craft, 144 people had been charged and imprisoned, and 20 had been executed. This memorial in Danvers lists the names of those who died because of the trials.

For the most part, officials and the general public held a naive faith that the witch trials must have been fair because they were guided by the hand of God. Even at the beginning of the Salem Witch Trials, however, a few people had had serious misgivings about the trials. Their reservations centered on the type of evidence used to accuse and convict suspected witches. As the trials continued, these doubts began to spread.

It Could Never Happen

"It has never yet been known that an innocent person has been punished on suspicion of witchcraft, and there is no doubt that God will never permit such a thing to happen."

Jakob Sprenger and Heinrich Kramer, Malleus Maleficarum, *1486*

Judge Saltonstall

One of the first and most important people to cast doubt on the trials was Nathaniel Saltonstall, a member of the Court of Oyer and Terminer. He resigned after the hanging of Bridget Bishop, claiming he was "very much dissatisfied with the proceedings of it." After resigning, Saltonstall was accused of being a witch, though he was never charged or arrested.

Doubts About Specters

Governor Phips had doubts about the fairness of the proceedings and concerns about spectral evidence. Early on in the trials, he wrote to minister Cotton Mather, son of Increase Mather, seeking guidance on the subject. In a reply on June 15, 1692, Mather and a dozen other ministers advised judges to be wary of evidence involving specters. The letter said that "there is a need of a very critical and exquisite caution" concerning "things received only upon the Devil's authority."

The Executions Continue

Neither the letter nor growing public concern could slow the pace of the trials and executions, which were watched by many people. One execution that created high drama was that of George Burroughs. Before being hanged August 19, he stunned witnesses by flawlessly reciting the Lord's Prayer. Superstition held that witches and wizards could not do so without stumbling over the words.

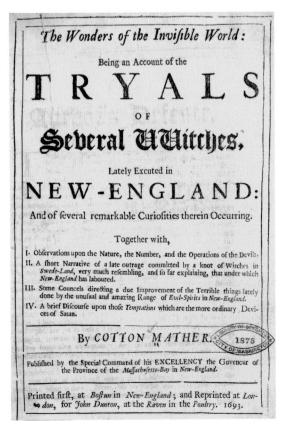

Cotton Mather may have questioned spectral evidence, but he was a firm believer in the evil of witches. He wrote this account of the Salem Witch Trials, saying the whole episode was the work of the devil.

Increase Mather (1639—1723) and Cotton Mather (1663—1728)

Increase Mather and his son Cotton Mather were two of New England's most important Puritan ministers and leaders. Both men were very strict, old-fashioned Puritans, and they believed that many of the bad things that happened in New England, including witchcraft, were due to the sins of its residents.

Increase Mather was minister of Boston's South Church from 1664 until the end of his life as well as the president of Harvard College from 1685 to 1701. These positions made him very

Cotton Mather prays to save an afflicted woman from witchcraft.

influential in New England society. He was also instrumental in negotiating a new charter for Massachusetts just before the witch trials.

Cotton Mather is famous for having written more than four hundred books and pamphlets, and some of his writings helped feed the fear of witches in Massachusetts that led to the incidents in Salem. Cotton Mather did, however, further the causes of education, science, and medicine in New England and helped to found Yale University.

Father and son at first supported the convictions in the Salem Witch Trials. As time went by, however, both men, but especially Increase Mather, expressed doubts about spectral evidence and questioned the justice of the trials.

More Doubts

After the August trials and executions, more people began to criticize spectral evidence. Robert Pike, an official who had helped collect evidence against suspected witches, wrote of his concerns to magistrate Jonathan Corwin of the Court of Oyer and Terminer. Pike was worried about the validity of testimony regarding "diabolical visions [and] apparitions."

One reason people believed there were witches was that so many had confessed. However, the public began to learn that some people in prison confessed only after being tortured.

A woman reads the Bible in a Puritan jail. Many of the accused were extremely devout Puritans.

Prison and Torture

The jails that housed those accused of being witches were terrible places. One of the worst was the Salem Jail, which was cold, dirty, and infested by rats. The accused were all kept in chains, including five-year-old Dorcas Good, who was so tiny that special chains had to be made. Torture was a practice allowed in Puritan New England, and the accused were sometimes tortured to make them confess. One method was to tie a rope to a person's neck and feet and draw them tight to cause the person great pain. Prisoners were fed salted foods and water mixed with pickled herring juice. The salty food and drink created a constant, dreadful thirst that was supposed to make them more likely to confess to their alleged crimes.

In spite of all the doubts, the executions continued: eight more accused witches were hanged in September 1692. This print shows the hanging of several women at one time.

Increase Mather Speaks Out

Six more people were condemned September 9, and nine more were found guilty September 17 in what was to be the final witch trial. The last hangings came September 22, 1692, when eight people, including Martha Corey and Mary Easty, were executed.

By this time, even more people had begun to believe the frenzy over witches had gone too far. Most were still afraid to speak out for fear that they, like past critics, would be charged with witchcraft. On October 3, 1692, however, Increase Mather delivered a sermon called "Cases of Conscience Concerning Evil Spirits." His powerful words against the use of spectral evidence helped lead to the end of the witch trials. His sermon concluded, "It were better that ten suspected witches should escape than one innocent person should be condemned."

The Trials End

Mather's powerful argument worked quickly. On October 12, 1692, Governor Phips ordered an end to the trials, and on October 29 he dissolved the Court of Oyer and Terminer. Phips wrote that he acted because "I saw many innocent persons might otherwise perish." Of the eleven people still awaiting execution, only two who died in jail lost their lives; the rest were eventually pardoned or freed.

Phips then appointed a new court to try the remaining cases. Although there were three more convictions, Phips granted them all **reprieves** from being hanged. In May 1693, the governor ordered the release of all accused witches still in prison. The Salem Witch Trials were finally over.

Puritan minister Increase Mather's "Cases of Conscience Concerning Evil Spirits" was one of several factors that brought the Witch Trails to an end.

A Black Cloud

"The black cloud that threatened this Province with destruction [has ended]; . . . this delusion of the Devil did spread and its dismal effects touched the lives and estates of many of their Majesty's Subjects and the reputation of some of the principal persons here . . ."

Governor Phips, letter to officials in England, October 12, 1692

Making Amends

Delusion of the Devil

The fear and strange incidents that led to the Salem Witch Trials are sometimes referred to as the "witchcraft **delusion**." When the horror of the accusations and trials finally ended, New Englanders tried to understand how they could have believed that their friends and neighbors, many of them good and kind people, could have been witches.

One view was that the devil had deluded them with specters. Juror Thomas Fiske claimed he and other members of the juries were simply "not capable to understand, nor able to withstand, the mysterious delusions of the Powers of Darkness and Prince of the Air [the devil]." This delusion theory became popular after the trials because it cleared the afflicted and those who convicted innocent people of any wrongdoing.

Later Theories

Historians since then have come up with more reasonable theories for the horror the witch trials created. The main theory is that

This cemetery in Salem dates from the time of the witch trials and is where Judge Hathorne is buried. Hathorne was one of many who let his fear and prejudice overrule his common sense.

A Change in Colonial Society

The Salem Witch Trials were caused in part by the strict intolerance Puritans had for anyone who failed to conform. However, this brutal intolerance began to soften in the decades following the trials. This was partly due to the shameful role church leaders had played in the trials, which undermined many Puritans' unquestioning faith in their church. Also, as the Massachusetts Bay Colony's population grew, so did other influences in the colony. Colonists began to rebel against church control by creating new communities that were more liberal in their attitudes. Even the church itself began to change as new religious ideas began to soften its harsh, strict views. These factors all combined to weaken Puritan control of New England.

people were infected with a sense of mass **hysteria**. The terrible fear people had of witches probably robbed them of their ability to reason clearly and make good judgments when the accusations began. This hysteria grew ever stronger and affected increasing numbers of people as the accusations mounted.

The cause of the hysteria was the initial charges made by several young girls, and it will never be known why they made such terrible accusations. Some people claim the girls' silly behavior and allegations began as a joke and that they had to keep making up new tales to avoid being punished for having lied in the first place.

Captain John Alden, who was accused of being a witch but fled to New York until the trials ended, believed that was the truth. He described the afflicted as "wenches who played their juggling tricks, falling down, crying out, and staring into peoples' faces."

Others have written that the girls could have been mentally ill or even have suffered physical problems that caused hallucinations of some kind. One theory claims that spoiled food, something common in that period, could have affected their minds and caused them to see strange things, which they then interpreted as visits by witches.

An illustration shows John Alden being accused of witchcraft by a child. A founder of Plymouth and leading citizen of Massachusetts, he believed the whole thing started as mischief and had nothing to do with the devil or witches.

Day of Repentance
"We do hereby signify to all in general (and to the surviving sufferers in especial) our deep sense of, and sorrow for, our errors in acting on such evidence to the condemning of any person. [We] hereby declare that we justly fear that we were sadly deluded and mistaken."

Massachusetts Bay Colony resolution ordering a day of repentance on January 16, 1697

Seeking Forgiveness

No matter what triggered the events of 1692, many people involved in the accusations, trials, and executions later felt a deep sense of shame and remorse. They realized their actions had led to the deaths of innocent people.

Five years after the trials, the Massachusetts Bay Colony ordered a day of **repentance**, but colonial leaders may have acted out of fear rather than repentance. Their resolution claimed God had been punishing them for the witch trials ever since, by "diminishing our substance, cutting short our harvest, blasting our most promising undertakings" and taking away loved ones "by sudden and violent deaths." Ann Putnam, a chief accuser, was one of the few afflicted who apologized, claiming she had been deluded by the devil.

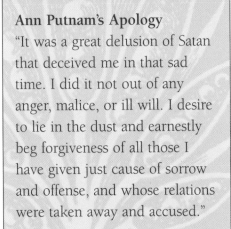

The Accused

It was difficult, if not impossible, for the accused who survived to return to a normal life. Many of them stayed in prison for months after the charges against them had been dropped because they could not afford to pay the fine required to cover the cost of housing and feeding them. For example, Lydia Dustin, acquitted in early March 1693, was still in prison when she died in mid-March because she did not have money for the fine. And Tituba Indian, the first accused, was the last released because Reverend Parris would not pay her fine. She was eventually sold to cover the cost of keeping her in jail for over a year.

Ann Putnam's Apology

"It was a great delusion of Satan that deceived me in that sad time. I did it not out of any anger, malice, or ill will. I desire to lie in the dust and earnestly beg forgiveness of all those I have given just cause of sorrow and offense, and whose relations were taken away and accused."

Ann Putnam, August 1706

Samuel Sewall, a judge in the Court of Oyer and Terminer, repents in public for his actions. He continued to observe a day of prayer each year to make amends for what he had done.

Many of the accused had also been ruined financially because their land, livestock, and other possessions had been seized by officials or stolen by citizens. And the lives of many people had been torn apart or damaged in other ways by the accusations.

Seeking Compensation

One of the hardest-hit families was that of the Goods. William Good, the husband of the executed Sarah Good and father of the the accused child Dorcas and the baby who died in prison, wrote the courts in 1710 to complain that the trials had caused the

Family Shame

Nathaniel Hawthorne is one of the most famous American novelists of the nineteenth century. His last name was really Hathorne, and his great-grandfather was John Hathorne, a magistrate during the Witch Trials. Hathorne was one of the most aggressive of the early officials involved in the Witch Trials. His combative questioning of Tituba Indian and other accused witches helped create the

Nathaniel Hawthorne in the 1860s.

accusatory tone that dominated the proceedings. The author was so appalled at his ancestor's central role in the trials that he altered his name by adding a "w" to it. In the introduction to his famous work *The Scarlet Letter*, Hawthorne wrote that he was willing to "take shame upon" himself for the things his great-grandfather had done.

"destruction of my poor family." Good's letter was one of many petitions to the colony by the accused and family members seeking compensation for what had happened to them. Although most of them received nothing, the Massachusetts Bay Colony, after years of legal battles, finally paid sums of money in 1712 to several victims.

Continuing To Make Amends

Nearly 250 years after the trials, descendants of some of the accused complained that their ancestors had never been fully absolved of their alleged crimes. In 1957, the Massachusetts General Court issued a resolution about the witch trials. The court declared that "no disgrace or cause for distress attaches to the said descendants or any of them by reason of said proceedings."

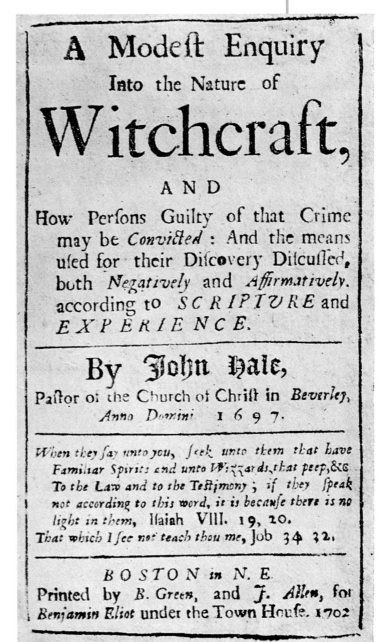

After the Salem Witch Trials, Massachusetts pastor John Hale wrote *A Modest Enquiry into the Nature of Witchcraft*. The book said that the mistakes made should be acknowledged so they didn't happen again.

In Due Time

". . . I fear not but the Lord in his due time will make me white as snow."

John Willard, one of the executed accused, May 1692

Conclusion

A high priestess of the Sacred Source congregation performs a Wiccan ritual. The group's ceremonies are far removed from traditional images of witchcraft—they have to do with spreading tolerance and love as well as celebrating spring.

Modern Witches

No one today fears the evil powers of witches because they know they are not real. Those few who claim to be witches are believers in a modern pagan religion called Wicca, a faith not recognized by Christians, Jews, or Muslims. The word comes from *wicce*, the old English word for witch. Wicca honors nature in festivals tied to the seasons. Although some Wiccans claim magical powers, their religion prohibits them from using magic to harm humans or other creatures. This unusual faith does not have many followers, but small groups of Wiccans exist in many countries, including the United States.

Danvers, Massachusetts

These modern witches are safe from the superstitious fear that three centuries ago resulted in the Salem Witch Trials. Today in Danvers, Massachusetts, the people who tragically lost their lives because of such fears are remembered as victims.

Danvers, which changed its name in 1752 from Salem Village to rid itself of its association with the witch trials, is home to the Salem Witch Memorial. The memorial was dedicated in 1992 to the accused who were executed or died in prison. The granite slabs bearing their names are a lasting reminder of how fear and accusations can lead to tragic consequences.

The Legacy of the Salem Witch Trials

The legacy of the Salem Witch Trials can be summed up in a single powerful term: witch-hunt. Today, the term refers to the injustice that occurs when innocent people are falsely accused of crimes in an atmosphere of fear, prejudice, and hysteria. This term was used in the 1940s and 1950s when Senator Joseph McCarthy led a campaign against alleged communists in the United States. In the process, he exploited

"Witch-hunt" leader Joseph McCarthy (right in light suit) presided at hearings reminiscent of the Salem Witch Trials.

Americans' fears and intolerance, whipping up an atmosphere of hatred. Eventually sense prevailed, and McCarthy lost his credibility just as the accusers had done in Salem, but not before much suffering was caused. The episode reminded people of the Salem Witch Trials, and we still use the term "witch-hunt" when hysterical accusations arise because of fear and prejudice today.

Time Line

1484	Edict approving witch-hunting is issued by Pope Innocent VIII.
1486	*Malleus Maleficarum* is published.
1542	Witchcraft is banned in England.
1604	Witchcraft Act makes witchcraft punishable by death in England.
1620	First Puritans come to North America and found Plymouth Colony.
1626	Salem Town is founded.
1630	Massachusetts Bay Colony is officially founded.
1630s	Settlement of Salem Village begins.
1686	Massachusetts charter is revoked by English king.
1689	November: Reverend Samuel Parris becomes pastor of Salem Village.
1691	New charter for Massachusetts is granted by King William III.
1692	February 29: Tituba Indian, Sarah Good, and Sarah Osborne are charged with being witches.
	March–April: First accused witches are questioned and sent to prison. Others in Salem Village are accused of being witches.
	Twenty-three more suspects are imprisoned.
	May: Thirty-nine more people are arrested for witchcraft.
	May 27: Governor William Phips appoints Court of Oyer and Terminer.
	June 2: Bridget Bishop is found guilty and hanged June 10.
	June 29–30: Five more accused are found guilty and hanged July 19.
	August 2–6: Six people are found guilty; five are hanged August 19.
	September 9: Six more accused are tried and sentenced to death.
	September 19: Giles Corey is pressed to death.
	September 17: Nine more are sentenced to death.
	September 22: Eight are hanged in the last executions.
	October 3: Increase Mather questions use of spectral evidence.
	October 12: Phips issues an order stopping witch trials.
	October 29: Phips dissolves Court of Oyer and Terminer.
1693	May: Phips orders release of all accused witches.
1697	January 16: Massachusetts Bay Colony declares a day of repentance.
1712	Massachusetts pays money to victims of Salem Witch Trials.
1752	Salem Village changes its name to Danvers.
1957	Massachusetts General Court declares no disgrace is attached to descendants of accused.
1992	Salem Witch Memorial is dedicated to victims of witch trials.

Glossary

afflicted: suffering or terribly distressed. This was the name given to those who were supposedly tormented by witches in Salem Village.

charter: legal document that grants land or powers. In the 1600s, the English king issued charters to groups of people wishing to set up colonies in the northeast of North America, a region then claimed by England. The colonies were ruled by a governor appointed in England.

colony: settlement, area, or country owned or controlled by another nation.

conformity: fitting in and following the accepted rules.

delusion: belief that is held even though it is not true.

edict: order or proclamation given by a leader.

epidemic: rapid spread of disease that affects a large number of people.

evidence: something used as proof, especially in a court of law.

hysteria: uncontrollable fear or excitement that causes unreasonable behavior, sometimes passing from one person to another.

jury: twelve people in a court who determine whether an accused person is guilty.

magistrate: local official who administers the law and acts as a judge in court cases.

meeting house: building in colonial America used for church services and town meetings.

New England: area of North America comprising colonies and later states of Maine, New Hampshire, Vermont, Massachusetts, Rhode Island, and Connecticut.

pagan: worshiping many gods or natural forces or both.

Protestant: Christian belonging to a group that separated from the Roman Catholic Church in the sixteenth century.

Puritan: person belonging to a Protestant Christian group that wanted to purify the Church of England. The word has since come to describe a person with very strict moral codes.

repentance: regret for wrongdoing and an intention to make amends or show remorse for wrong actions or thoughts.

reprieve: postponement of a sentence.

specter: visible spirit or ghost.

testify: give evidence at a trial.

testimony: words of a person given in evidence at a trial.

trial: legal process of proving or disproving, in a court of law, a case in which someone has been accused of a crime.

try: conduct a trial.

witchcraft: use of magical powers and practice of witch's rituals.

Further Information

Books

Barenblatt, Rachel and Jean Craven. *Massachusetts: The Bay State* (World Almanac Library of the States). World Almanac Library, 2002.

Collier, Christopher and James Lincoln Collier. *Pilgrims and Puritans: 1620–1676* (Drama of American History). Marshall Cavendish, 1998.

Furbee, Mary Rodd. *Outrageous Women of Colonial America*. John Wiley & Sons, 2001.

Hakim, Joy. *Making Thirteen Colonies* (History of US). Oxford University Press, 1999.

Kallen, Stuart A. *Witches* (The Mystery Library). Lucent, 2000.

Stein, Wendy. *Witches: Opposing Viewpoints* (Great Mysteries). Greenhaven Press, 1995.

Wilson, Lori Lee. *The Salem Witch Trials* (How History Is Invented). Lerner, 1998.

Web Sites

www.etext.lib.virginia.edu/salem/witchcraft Transcripts of most of the court proceedings in the Salem Witch Trials and good images from the University of Virginia.

www.nationalgeographic.com/features/97/salem Interactive feature about the Salem Witch Trials from National Geographic.

www.salemwitchtrials.com Background to and interesting facts about the Salem Witch Trials.

Useful Addresses

Salem Witch Museum
Washington Square
Salem, MA 01970
Telephone: (978) 744-1692

Index

Page numbers in *italics* indicate maps and diagrams. Page numbers in **bold** indicate other illustrations.